# HARK, HARK, THE LARK

*8 Shakespeare settings for upper voices*

Compiled and edited by Bob Chilcott

MUSIC DEPARTMENT

OXFORD

UNIVERSITY PRESS

# OXFORD

UNIVERSITY PRESS

Great Clarendon Street, Oxford OX2 6DP,
United Kingdom

Oxford University Press is a department of the University of Oxford.
It furthers the University's objective of excellence in research, scholarship,
and education by publishing worldwide. Oxford is a registered trade mark of
Oxford University Press in the UK and in certain other countries

First published 2015

Impression: 2

ISBN 978-0-19-340615-5

Music and text origination by
Katie Johnston
Printed in Great Britain on acid-free paper by
Halstan & Co. Ltd, Amersham, Bucks.

# Preface

In order to mark the four hundredth anniversary of the death of William Shakespeare, we have collected together eight newly composed settings of some of his most familiar words. Many singers all over the world will be familiar with so many of the songs in Shakespeare's plays through the work of composers such as Ralph Vaughan Williams, Gerald Finzi, Sir Michael Tippett, Frank Martin, and John Rutter, to name but a few. For this collection we have asked composers from Britain, Canada, the United States, Australia, and Finland to put their own stamp on Shakespeare's songs and texts—words that abound with energy and that have so much singing line and rhythm within them; words that, in fact, are in most cases surely meant to be sung.

Our source for the texts, and for general reference, has been The Oxford Shakespeare edition, and we have been extremely lucky to have had guidance from Carol Rutter, Professor of Shakespeare and Performance Studies at Warwick University. I would also like to thank Philip Croydon, Commissioning Editor at Oxford University Press, for his support and guidance on this book, and also Robyn Elton and Laura Jones for their careful editing work.

In putting this collection together, I hope we have achieved our aim of creating a practical performance edition that can be used by choirs everywhere to celebrate the life and work of one of our greatest writers—as well as the music of some wonderful contemporary composers.

Bob Chilcott
June 2015

Also available from Oxford University Press:
*Shall I compare thee?: 10 Shakespeare settings for mixed voices* (978–0–19–340614–8)

# Contents

# And will he not come again?

William Shakespeare
from *Hamlet* (Act 4, Scene 5)

PAUL JARM
(b. 1

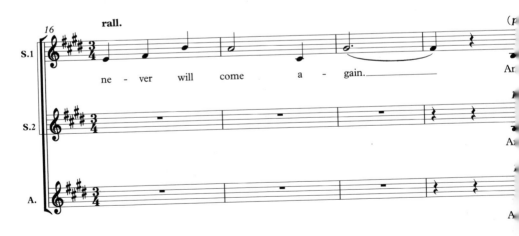

Duratic

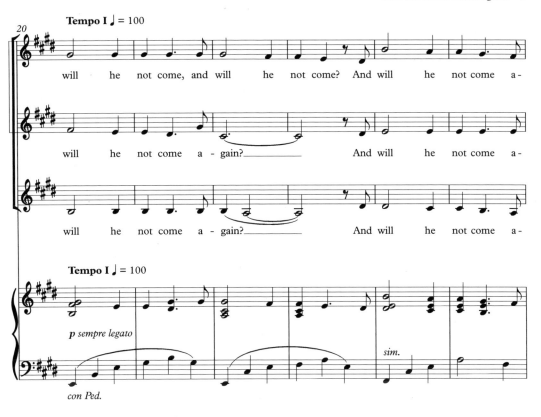

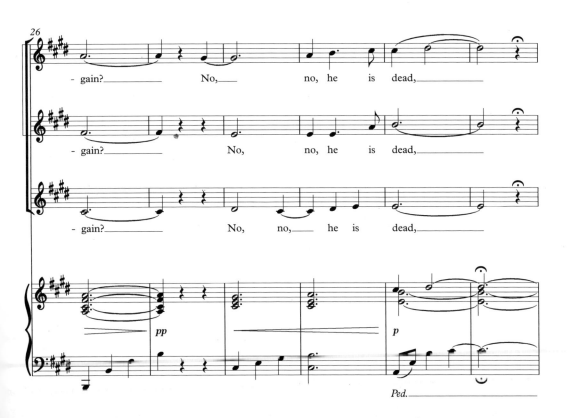

# Blow, blow, thou winter wind

William Shakespeare
from *As You Like It* (Act 2, Scene 7)

SARAH QUARTEL
(b. 1982)

Duration: 2.5 mins

freeze,_____ thou bit - ter sky,_____ That

freeze,_____ thou bit - ter sky,_____ That

dost not_____ bite_____ so nigh As

dost not_____ bite_____ so nigh As

be - ne - fits for - got._____

be - ne - fits for - got._____

*for Cheryl Dupont and the New Orleans Children's Chorus*

# Come unto these yellow sands

William Shakespeare
from *The Tempest* (Act 1, Scene 2)

BOB CHILCOTT
(b. 1955)

Duration: 1.5 mins

* *whist* = into silence

* *featly* = neatly and elegantly
† unpitched; bark like a dog
‡ *burden* = chorus

* *chanticleer* = a domestic cockerel

# Hark, hark, the lark

William Shakespeare
from *Cymbeline* (Act 2, Scene 3)

ALAN BULLARD
(b. 1947)

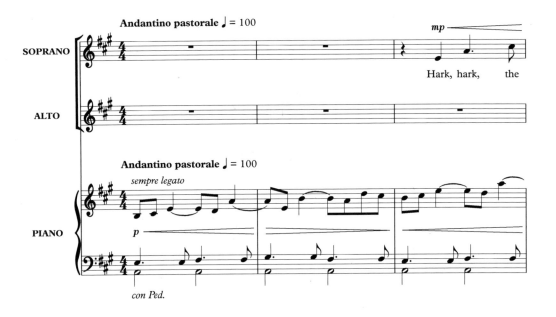

Duration: 2 mins

* *Phoebus* = Apollo, the sun-god
† *'gins* = begins to

* the bud of a marigold
† *ope* = open

*for Angie Johnson and the Young Naperville Singers*

# Our revels now are ended

William Shakespeare
from *The Tempest* (Act 4, Scene 1)

BOB CHILCOTT
(b. 1955)

Duration: 3 mins

* *rack* = cloud or mist driven by the wind
† *on* = of

# Over hill, over dale

William Shakespeare
from *A Midsummer Night's Dream* (Act 2, Scene 1)

ANDREA RAMSEY

Duration: 3 mins

* *tho-rough* = through. The standard early modern spelling of the word, indicating pronunciation in two syllables.

* *pale* = an area of land enclosed by a wooden fence

Swift - er than the moon - ës sphere,

Swift - er than the moon - ës sphere,

S./A.

And I serve the Fai - ry Queen To

dew her orbs u - pon the

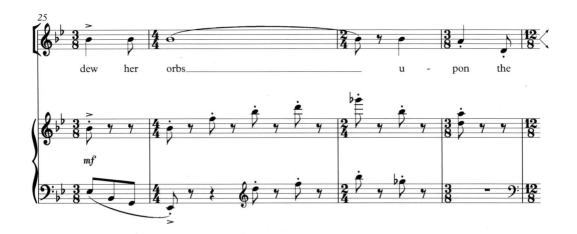

* *pensioners* = the title of Queen Elizabeth's royal bodyguard

* *savours* = fragrance

* *lob* = country bumpkin, clown, or lout

O - ver park, o - ver pale,

Tho-rough flood, tho-rough fire;

*mf* *ff*

S. I do wan - der ev - 'ry - where

A. I do wan - der ev - 'ry - where

*mf* *dim.* *mp*

Swift – er than the moon-ës sphere,

Swift – er than the moon-ës sphere,____

**S./A.**

And I serve the Fai – ry Queen To

dew her orbs____ u – pon the

green.

# When icicles hang by the wall

William Shakespeare
from *Love's Labour's Lost* (Act 5, Scene 2)

STEPHEN HATFIELD
(b. 1956)

Duration: 2.5 mins

All stage directions are optional.

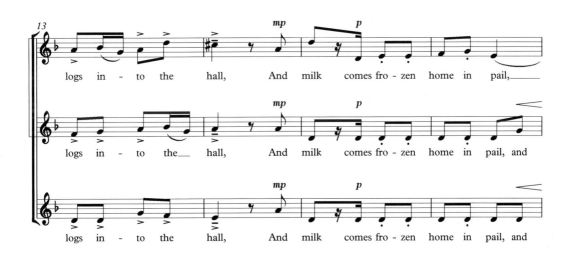

* *blows his nail* = warms his hands by blowing on them

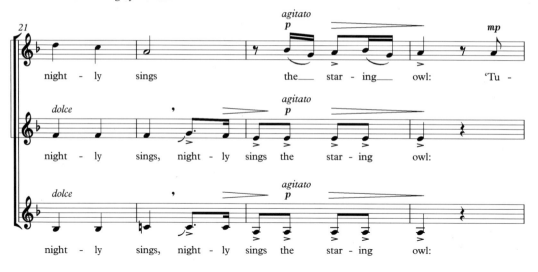

* *keel* = to stir the pot and scrape the inner sides to prevent it boiling over

[1] stage direction: 'ha!' indicates that singers should give a rheumy, phlegmy cough
[2] stage direction: 'Marian' blows her nose
* *saw* = sermon

³ stage direction: 'Marian' gives an even louder honk
⁴ stage direction: some or all singers warm their hands over the bowl
\* *crabs* = crab-apples

a mer-ry___ note, While greas-y Joan doth keel___ the
mer-ry___ note,___
___ A mer-ry note, While greas-y Joan doth keel___ the

pot, while greas-y Joan doth keel___ the pot, keel___ the
While greas-y Joan doth keel___ the pot, keel___ the
pot, while greas-y Joan doth keel___ the pot, keel___ the

**Meno mosso**

'Tu - whit, Tu - whoo!'___    Tu - whit,    Tu - whoo!'___

pot.    'Tu - whit, Tu - whoo!'___
pot.    'Tu - whit, Tu-whoo!    Tu - whit, Tu - whoo!'___
pot.    'Tu - whit, Tu-whoo!'___

# You spotted snakes with double tongue

William Shakespeare
from *A Midsummer Night's Dream* (Act 2, Scene 2)

JUSSI CHYDENIUS
(b. 1972)

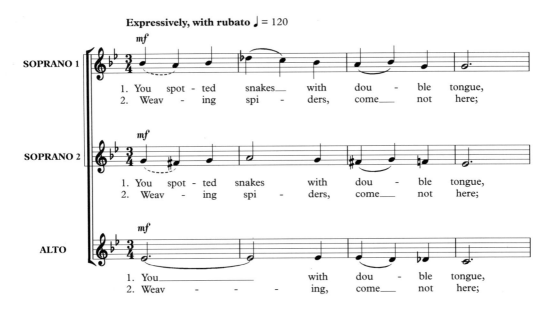

Duration: 2.5 mins

**poco rall.**

do — no wrong; Come not near our Fai - ry Queen.
-proach not near;— Worm nor — snail do no— of - fence.

do no wrong;— Come not near our Fai - ry Queen.
-proach not near;— Worm nor snail do no of - fence.

do no wrong;— Come not near our Fai - ry Queen.
-proach not near;— Worm nor snail do no— of - fence.

**Angelically** ♩ = 100

Phil - o - mel* with mel - o - dy,— Sing in our sweet lul - la - by;—

Phil - o - mel* with mel - o - dy, Sing in our sweet lul - la - by;—

Phil - o - mel* with mel - o - dy, Sing— in our— sweet lul - la - by;—

Lul - la, lul - la, lul - la - by; lul - la, lul - la, lul - la - by.

Lul - la, lul - la, lul - la - by; lul - la, lul - la, lul - la - by.—

Lul - la, lul - la, lul - la - by;— lul - la, lul - la, lul - la - by.

* *Philomel* = a nightingale. Shakespeare references Ovid's *Metamorphosis*, in which the character Philomela is transformed i
a nightingale.

**poco accel.**     **poco rall.**

*cresc.*     *f*

Ne-ver harm    Nor spell nor charm    Come our love - ly la - dy nigh._____

*cresc.*     *f*

Ne - ver harm,_____    nor charm___    Come our love - ly la - dy nigh._____

*cresc.*     *f*

Ne-ver harm    Nor spell nor charm    Come our love - ly la - dy nigh._____

**1.**

**a tempo**     **poco rall.**

*mp dolce*

So good night    with    lul  -  la  -  by._____

*mp dolce*

So good night_____    with    lul  -  la  -  by._____

*mp dolce*

So good night    with_____ lul  -  la  -  by,_____ lul-la- by.

**2.**

**Slower**     **rall.**

*p dolce*

So good night,    with    lul  -  la  -  by._____

*p dolce*

So good night,_____    with    lul  -  la  -  by._____

*p dolce*

So good - night    with_____ lul  -  la,    lul - la - by.